Evergreen

Copyright © 2015 SweetGeorgieAnnsBooksandWhatNot
www.sweetgeorgieannsbooksandwhatnot.com

Text and Photos © (Barbara) Barbie DelCamp

All rights Reserved
ISBN 978-0-9912642-7-8

Library of Congress control number:2015918950

No part of this work may be reproduced or transmitted in any form or by any means, electronically or mechanically, including photocopying, matting or framing any pages from this book (with the intent to create other products for sale or resale for profit) and recording, or by any information storage or retrival system, except as may be expressly permitted by the 1976 Copyright Act or by writing from the publisher.

Evergreen

This book is dedicated to the wonderful people that take care of Evergreen Cemetery.
It is also dedicated to the people who frequently go to Evergreen to walk and enjoy the property.
It has been a pleasure to meet so many gentlemen, ladies, and families who have a long history and tradition of respectfully appreciating the wildlife there.

Bertram called her
Chloe
but most knew them
as
Mr. and Mrs.
Montgomery
who loved one
another dearly.

It was here that Chloe laid her eggs in a nest, near some mallard ducks and on top of a ledge.

Bert swam
and
ate where he could
still see her,
along a green hedge.

One early morning at dawn the eggs started hatching. Before long, the little goslings could be seen.

At Evergreen that day
there was a quiet
"hush"
over the water,
gentle and serene.

Making their way into the world
appeared small puffy birds
with feathers a
yellowish
colored cream.

Moving slowly at first, the goslings yawned as their mother hovered over them keeping them safe and sound.

To the right of
Mrs. Montgomery,
a duck flew in.
She too was
waiting for the day
when her chicks would
hatch near that same
ground.

Bertram watched
as the goslings
stirred about
and
attempted to stand
on their
teeny feet.

The babies looked
to Chloe
and
followed her lead
to the edge
of the ledge.
Watching them
toddle was funny
and
sweet.

Looking at the water one gosling's face seemed to shout… "say what? You want me to jump…?" as it turned its head to see what was below.

One by one the babies leapt into the pond. For those of us watching it was a special and delightful show.

Together as a family,
they started swimming around.
The goslings were cute as could be
as they waddled out of the pool...

and under a stump that they found. Bert, the proud father lifted his neck and let them all run swiftly past. He was always alert to danger and regularly waited to be last.

The sun set
and
the moon rose
as the
young Montgomerys
grew quite fast.

From the shore, they looked on as the tiny ducklings were finally born.

There in the grass the goslings rested whenever they felt tired and worn.

Most days the geese heard the great egret make the sound, "cuk, cuk, cuk" when it flew to the water looking for fish.

For the stunning
white egret
it was its favorite dish.

Over time the goslings' wings grew wide and long. Soon they were flapping them, they were so strong.

The young birds used them to glide on the pond.

Their time together created an intimate bond.

They practiced their flying
and
enjoyed the breeze.

Overhead was the sound of honking and
jubilee as many other geese gathered in the sky calling to the Montgomerys.

"Come join us!"
high
above
the
trees.

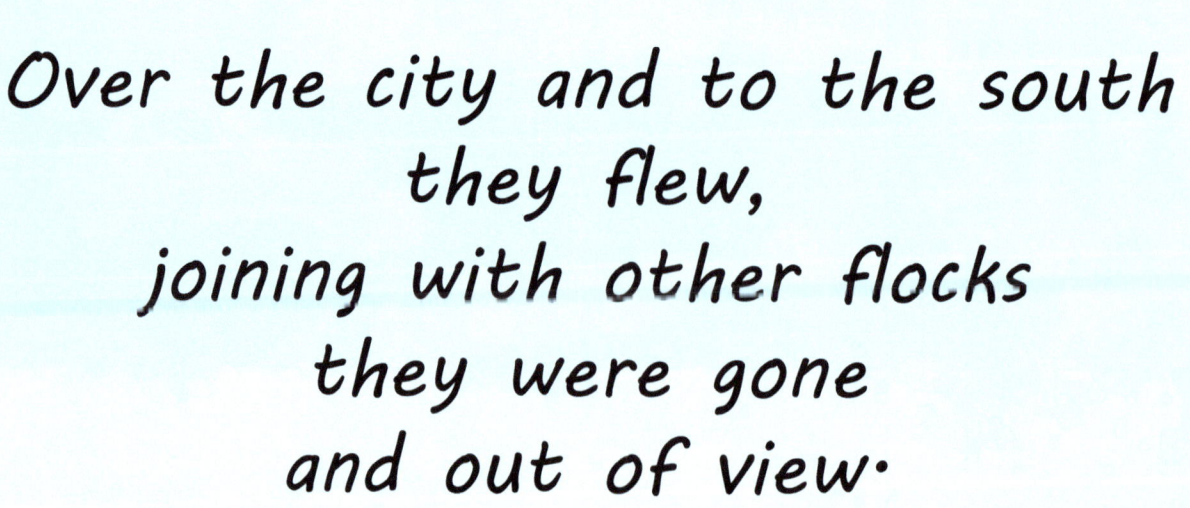

Over the city and to the south
they flew,
joining with other flocks
they were gone
and out of view.

Did you know?

A female goose lays one egg a day until all of her eggs are in the nest.

A gander is a male goose.

Goslings are baby geese.

Geese are very strong and protective of their family.

Always approach them with caution.

It takes 2-3 months before goslings are ready to fly.

Canada geese are the largest of all geese.

A gander helps to raise goslings but a male mallard does not help to raise ducklings.

Molting is when geese and ducks lose their feathers and grow new ones.

Geese and ducks molt once a year.

www.ingramcontent.com/pod-product-compliance
Lightning Source LLC
Chambersburg PA
CBHW041127300426
44113CB00003B/91